NORTHERN SKY

This star map has the North Celestial Pole at its center. It shows constellations of the northern sky. Constellations lying across the celestial equator appear on both maps. Paler areas represent the Milky Way.

Constellations of the northern sky featured in this book:

Ursa Major ∞ the Great Bear

Ursa Minor ∞ the Little Bear

Cygnus ∞ the Swan

Vulpecula ∞ the Fox

Leo ∞ the Lion

Taurus ∞ the Bull

Gemini ∞ the Twins

Draco ∞ the Dragon

+ marks the Celestial Pole

SOUTHERN SKY

This star map has the South Celestial Pole at its center. It shows constellations of the southern sky. Constellations lying across the celestial equator appear on both maps. Paler areas represent the Milky Way.

Pegasus

Cetus

Mira

Taurus

Phoenix

Fomalhaut

Aquarius

Grus

Altair

Eridanus

Achernar

Tucana

Capricornus

Aquila

Orion

Rigel

Dorado

Hydrus

Pavo

Sagittarius

Serpens Cauda

Columba

Betelgeuse

Lepus

Canopus

Volans

+Apus

Ara

Carina

Musca

TriA *

Ophiuchus

Sirius

Rigil Kent

Antares

Canis Major

Vela

Crux

Lupus

Puppis

Centaurus

Scorpius

Procyon

Libra

Canis Minor

Serpens Caput

Hydra

Corvus

Spica

Regulus

Virgo

*TriA=Triangulum Australe

+ marks the Celestial Pole

Constellations of the southern sky featured in this book:

Scorpius ∞ the Scorpion

Lupus ∞ the Wolf

Canis Major ∞ the Great Dog

Lepus ∞ the Hare

Dorado ∞ the Goldfish

Volans ∞ the Flying Fish

Cetus ∞ the Whale

Pavo ∞ the Peacock

Apus ∞ the Bird of Paradise

Tucana ∞ the Toucan

Grus ∞ the Crane

TO MY MOTHER, WHO TAUGHT ME TO LOVE BOOKS AND THE STARS ✦ J.M.

FOR MY GUARDIAN ANGEL, SARAH SLACK ✦ C.B.

Zoo in the Sky copyright © 1998 Frances Lincoln Limited
Text copyright © 1998 Jacqueline Mitton
Illustrations copyright © 1998 Christina Balit
Star maps by Wil Tirion

First paperback printing 2006

ISBN-10: 0-7922-5935-1
ISBN-13: 978-0-7922-5935-0

Published by the National Geographic Society
1145 17th Street N.W.
Washington, D.C. 20036

First published in the United Kingdom in 1998 by
Frances Lincoln Limited, 4 Torriano Mews,
Torriano Avenue, London NW5 2RZ

Library of Congress Catalog Card Number: 97-75429

The Society is supported through the membership
dues and income from the sale of its educational
products. Call 1-800-NGS-LINE for more
information or visit our website at
www.nationalgeographic.com

Printed in China
20/QT/13
13

Zoo in the Sky

A Book of Animal Constellations

Jacqueline Mitton

Pictures by Christina Balit

◻ NATIONAL GEOGRAPHIC SOCIETY

Washington, D.C.

W HEN THE SUN

sets, darkness falls. The stars appear one by one. Then the sky turns to a picture puzzle. What is hiding in the patterns of stars? Some people say they only see squares and squiggles, lines and loops. But imagine hard, and the sky comes to life. The star patterns make a wing here, a tail there, a twinkling eye, even a scorpion's stinger. Sky watchers long, long ago imagined a whole zoo of animals. They shine there still when you are under the magic spell of the nighttime sky.

THE GREAT BEAR

quietly pads her way around the North Pole of the sky. Every day she makes the trip. Two bright stars across her back point straight to Polaris, the North Star. Hanging off Polaris by his tail, the Little Bear swings around behind her. You won't see bears quite the same anywhere else—real live bears don't have long tails!

COUNTLESS STARS

light the Milky Way. Along this silvery path, with wings outstretched, flies the Swan. On July and August nights, he soars from east to west across the sky. It takes him from dusk till dawn. His eye gleams with a twin star, yellow and blue, called Albireo. He needs a good eye to keep a sharp lookout. The cunning Fox runs beneath him, looking for his dinner.

THE SCORPION has a nasty sting in his tail. Beware as he scuttles across the Milky Way. His tail is curved around and he is waving his fearsome claws. Antares, a blood-red star, glows at his heart. But the Wolf nearby is not afraid. After all, he is not such a friendly creature himself.

LEO THE LION is king of the beasts and lord of the sky. In February and March he looks down from a throne high up in the heavens. Stars in his mane shine like jewels in a crown. His brightest star lies close to his heart. That star's name is Regulus, which means "the little king."

CHARGING through the zodiac, here comes the Bull. Head down, horns thrust forward, Taurus is ready to toss the Twins. But they are safe, always on the other side of the Milky Way. The Bull glowers with a brilliant red eye, the star Aldebaran. A whole cluster of stars is scattered around his nose. The Pleiades huddle behind his shoulder. These starry sisters are not afraid. They know he never looks back.

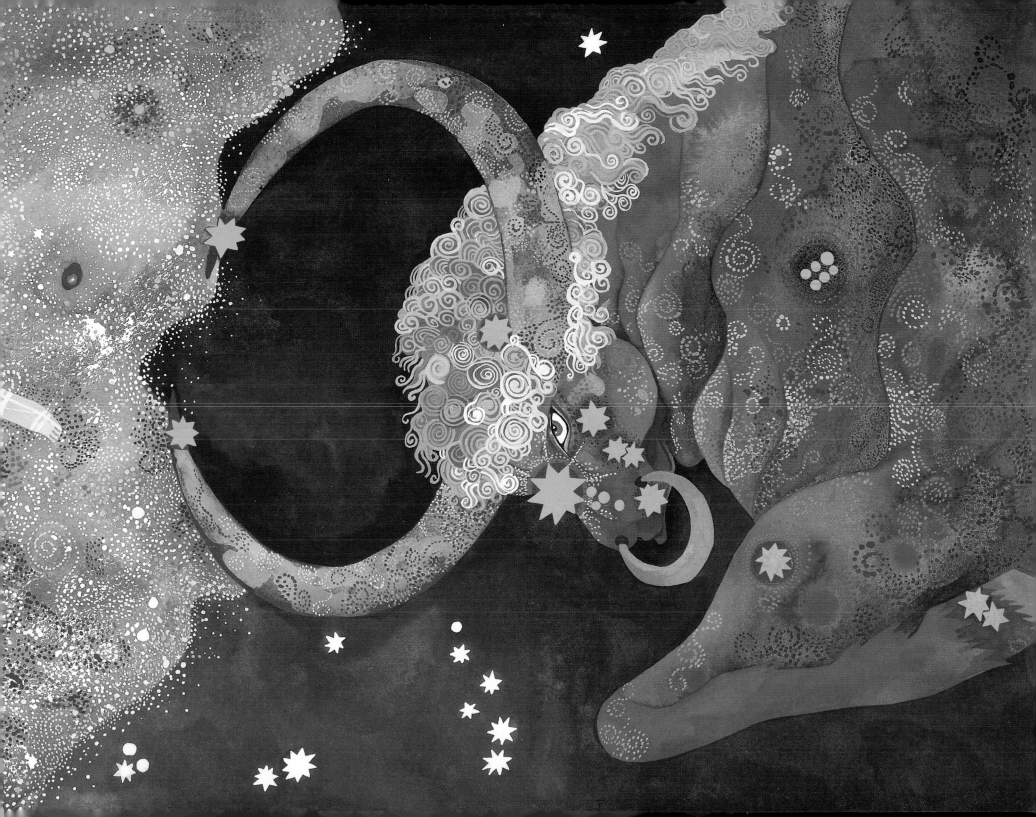

THE GREAT DOG is chasing the Hare but knows he never can catch it. This dog is a splendid, star-studded creature. His brightest star, Sirius, outshines all others in the night sky. Sirius means "scorching one"—a good name for a white-hot star. But spot it low in the sky, and Sirius flashes all the colors of the rainbow, like a diamond glinting in sunlight.

DEEP in the southern sky, the glittering Goldfish swims alongside where the good ship Argo sails an ocean of stars. The Flying Fish gives chase in fun, soaring out of the waves. "Now, take care," he warns. "We must not get caught." But the fish are safe in their starry sea. They will never be anyone's dinner.

THE WHALE is the greatest of all living creatures. He is one of the largest in the sky, too. A monstrous size, he is sometimes called the Sea Monster. On the Whale's back you find Mira, the marvelous star. See how red it glows by his fin. Mira keeps dimming till it disappears; then little by little it brightens once more. About a year later it's back, bright as ever, only to fade all over again.

A ZOO without birds would never do. In the sky there's a whole flock, parading by the South Pole. Tails on display, the proud Peacock and the Bird of Paradise show off to anyone who watches. The Toucan's glory is his beak, studded with an orange star. The Crane peers at them all, stretching his long neck. Red and blue stars shine on his back.

THE LONG, scaly body of the crimson-eyed Dragon coils around the North Pole of the heavens. Take care—he might breathe fire! You won't find a dragon like him in an ordinary zoo. But the starry sky is magic, and one fine sparkly night—who knows—you just might fall under its spell.

What are the stars?

Stars are giant balls of hot gas. They shine because they are so hot. The heat of a star comes from its center, which creates energy like a natural nuclear power station. Our Sun is a star. It is the only star in our Solar System. The other stars of the night sky look much fainter than the Sun, because they are at least 27,000 times farther from the Earth.

The sky above you

The Sun rises and sets daily because our Earth spins around on its axis once every 24 hours. Like the Sun, some stars rise in the east and set in the west. Each night, these stars rise about 4 minutes earlier than on the night before. This means that the constellations in the night sky gradually change, week by week, month by month. The constellations visible in summer cannot be seen in winter.

The stars in your sky also depend on where you are in the world. Unless you are on the Equator, some stars are always hidden below the horizon. If you are in Europe or North America, for example, you will never see the Peacock or the Southern Cross. If you are in Australia, you will never see the Great Bear or the Little Bear. Some stars, however, circle around the North or South Pole, and never set. They are visible all year round on clear nights by people far enough north or south to see them.

When you look at Earth maps, east is on the right and west on the left, but on sky maps it is the opposite. The pictures in this book follow sky maps. For example, the Swan, which seems to fly from east to west in the sky, flies left to right across the page.

The Sun, and all the stars you can see without a telescope, belong to a family of thousands of millions of stars that we call our Galaxy. On a clear, dark night, you can see the light from countless stars in our Galaxy concentrated in a misty band across the sky called the Milky Way. Beyond our own Galaxy, there are billions of other galaxies scattered through the universe.

The constellations

For as far back in time as records go, and probably long before then, people have imagined pictures in the star patterns and given them names. Today, astronomers divide the whole of the sky into 88 constellations, with official Latin names. Every star, however faint, is now included in one constellation or another.

Forty-eight of the constellations are very ancient. They were listed by the Greek astronomer Ptolemy in the second century A.D., but were used even earlier. Most of the others were added by people making star maps between 200 and 400 years ago.

Every year the Sun slowly moves in a circle around the sky, passing through the twelve constellations known as the zodiac: Aries, Taurus, Gemini, Cancer, Leo, Virgo, Libra, Scorpius, Sagittarius, Capricornus, Aquarius, and Pisces.

Some star patterns have their own popular names, although they are not whole constellations. The best known is the Plough or Big Dipper, which is made up of seven stars in the Great Bear constellation.

Nearly all the brighter stars in the night sky have individual names. Many of these names were given to them by the ancient Arab astronomers, and have a meaning in their language. For example, Aldebaran means "the follower."

NORTHERN SKY

This star map has the North Celestial Pole at its center. It shows constellations of the northern sky. Constellations lying across the celestial equator appear on both maps. Paler areas represent the Milky Way.

Constellations of the northern sky featured in this book:

Ursa Major ∾ the Great Bear

Ursa Minor ∾ the Little Bear

Cygnus ∾ the Swan

Vulpecula ∾ the Fox

Leo ∾ the Lion

Taurus ∾ the Bull

Gemini ∾ the Twins

Draco ∾ the Dragon

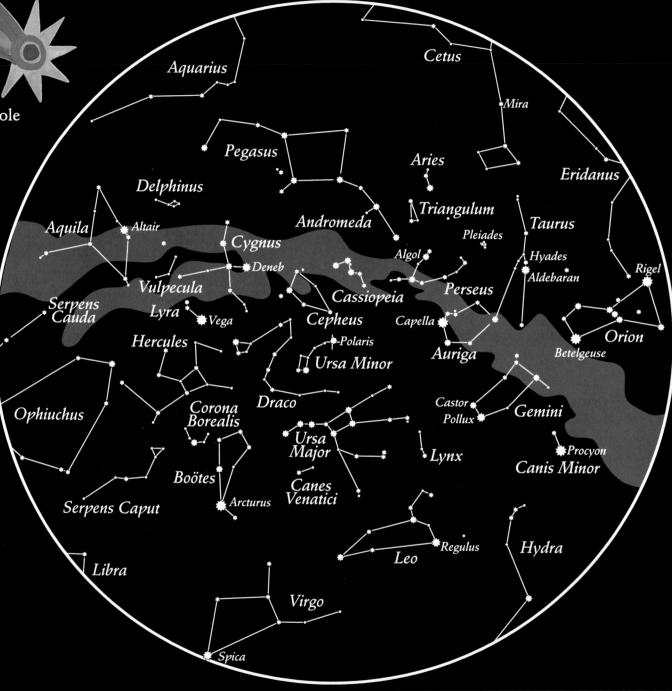

+ marks the Celestial Pole